TANGERINE

by
Edward Bloor

Teacher Guide

Written by
Stacie Lee Champlin Dreibrodt

Edited by
Monica L. Odle

Note

The Apple Signature edition of the book published by Scholastic Inc. ©1997 (first Scholastic paperback printing, September 1998) was used to prepare this guide. The page references may differ in other editions.

Please note: Please assess the appropriateness of this book for the age level and maturity of your students prior to reading and discussing it with your class.

ISBN 1-58130-668-7

Printed in the United States of America.

To order, contact your local school supply store, or—

Novel Units, Inc.
P.O. Box 433
Bulverde, TX 78163-0433

Web site: www.educyberstor.com

Table of Contents

Skills and Strategies

Thinking
Identifying attributes, research, compare/contrast

Comprehension
Predicting, cause/effect, problem solving, evaluating

Vocabulary
Target words, application, synonyms

Listening/Speaking
Class discussion, debate, small group discussion, drama

Literary Elements
Characterization, similes, metaphors, foreshadowing, symbolism

Writing
Journal, personal narrative, persuasive, letter, poem

Across the Curriculum
Science, media, physical education, history, art

Summary

Tangerine is a story comprised of the journal entries of Paul Fisher, a young man who stands in the shadow of his older brother, Erik, and his promising football career. While Paul's parents never miss one of Erik's football games, they only attend one of Paul's soccer matches. Everyone except Paul seems to be very interested in external appearances of things. Paul's mom strives to make the neighborhood architecturally pretty, even though the foundations are rotting away. She prefers to think of Erik as a football star and refuses to see that he is mean and cruel. Paul's dad is also blind to Erik's wrongdoings and is only concerned with getting Erik a college football scholarship. The truth soon catches up with the family. Paul discovers that his vision-impairment is a result of Erik's cruelty, and the police accuse Erik and his buddy Arthur, of both murder and theft. Throughout the novel, Paul also struggles with trying to fit in at a school where, at first, the people seem nothing like him. He begins to realize that he does fit in even though their houses and lifestyles are not the same. Paul, though almost blind, discovers the importance of seeing and living the truth, even if it isn't pleasant.

About the Author

Edward Bloor lives in Florida with his wife and children. He is a teacher at both the middle school and high school levels. *Tangerine* is Bloor's first novel and he is currently working on another novel for young readers. *Tangerine* has been recognized as one of the ALA Top Ten Best Books for Young Adults, a *Horn Book* Fanfare Book, An *American Bestseller* Pick of the List, a NYPL One Hundred Titles for Reading and Sharing, and *The Bulletin of the Center for Children's Books* Blue Ribbon Book.

Introductory Activities

1. Previewing the book: Have the students study the cover of the book. Ask them to respond to the following questions about what they see: who? what? where? when? why? Based on their answers, have the students predict what the novel will be about.

2. Given the following clues, students will write a paragraph predicting what they think will happen in the story.

   cruelty　　sibling rivalry　　loyalty　　friendship　　winning

3. Character Diary: Introduce the main character, Paul Fisher. Ask the students to pretend that they are Paul. After they finish reading each day, or as they go along, encourage them to write a diary entry from Paul's perspective. Have time for the students to share their entries with their classmates.

4. Create an attribute web (p. 5 of this guide) with students for each of the following ideas: friendship, loyalty, family, pride, status, and fear. Focus on one word at a time. Begin by writing the word in the center of a large piece of paper. Ask students to quickly tell what each word brings to mind. Encourage students to elaborate on particular ideas.

5. Prediction Chart: Have the students set up a prediction chart to use as they read the novel (pp. 6-7 of this guide).

6. Anticipation Questions: Have students respond to each of the following statements with a "thumbs-up" (I agree) or a "thumbs-down" (I disagree) and discuss their responses.
   - It is important to like yourself.
   - Young people should be punished for bad behavior.
   - You should always respect your older siblings.
   - Families should stick together.
   - Things truly are as they seem.
   - People never change.
   - It is always important to follow through on a promise.
   - It is impossible to improve your character.

7. Influences: Ask students how specific events helped to shape them into the person they are today. Ask them to think about what they might be like had the events never taken place.

Vocabulary Activities

1. Word Wall: Assign each student one or two words from the vocabulary list for the section of the book you are reading. Ask the students to look up the words in a dictionary and draw a picture that illustrates their word. They will then share the word and the drawing with the class. The students in the class will record the definition in their notebooks. The drawing and the word will be tacked up on a wall in the classroom.

2. Sentences: Have the students select five or six vocabulary words and use as many as possible in one sentence.

3. Synonym Match: Have students select vocabulary words from a section and list one synonym for each vocabulary word on a small piece of paper. Students mix the papers and match each synonym to the appropriate vocabulary word.

4. Vocabulary Sort: Have students sort the words into categories they choose. Then ask the students to share their reasoning with you and the class.

5. Vocabulary Around the World: Arrange the desks in a circle in the room. Have one less desk than students so that one student is always standing. Read a vocabulary word aloud. The standing student and the person sitting in the desk to his/her left compete to give the correct definition first. The first student to give the correct definition stands (or remains standing) and moves on to the next desk. The winning student rotates around the entire room defining every word correctly.

6. Vocabulary Charades: Place the vocabulary words in a basket. Have the students draw out a word and act it out for the class. This can be done individually, with a partner, or in small groups. You can also pick specific words from the novel not already included in the vocabulary lists.

Attribute Web

Using Predictions in the Novel Unit Approach

We all make predictions as we read—little guesses about what will happen next, how a conflict will be resolved, which details will be important to the plot, which details will help fill in our sense of a character. Students should be encouraged to predict, to make sensible guesses as they read the novel.

As students work on their predictions, these discussion questions can be used to guide them: What are some of the ways to predict? What is the process of a sophisticated reader's thinking and predicting? What clues does an author give to help us make predictions? Why are some predictions more likely to be accurate than others?

Create a chart for recording predictions. This could be either an individual or class activity. As each subsequent chapter is discussed, students can review and correct their previous predictions about plot and characters as necessary.

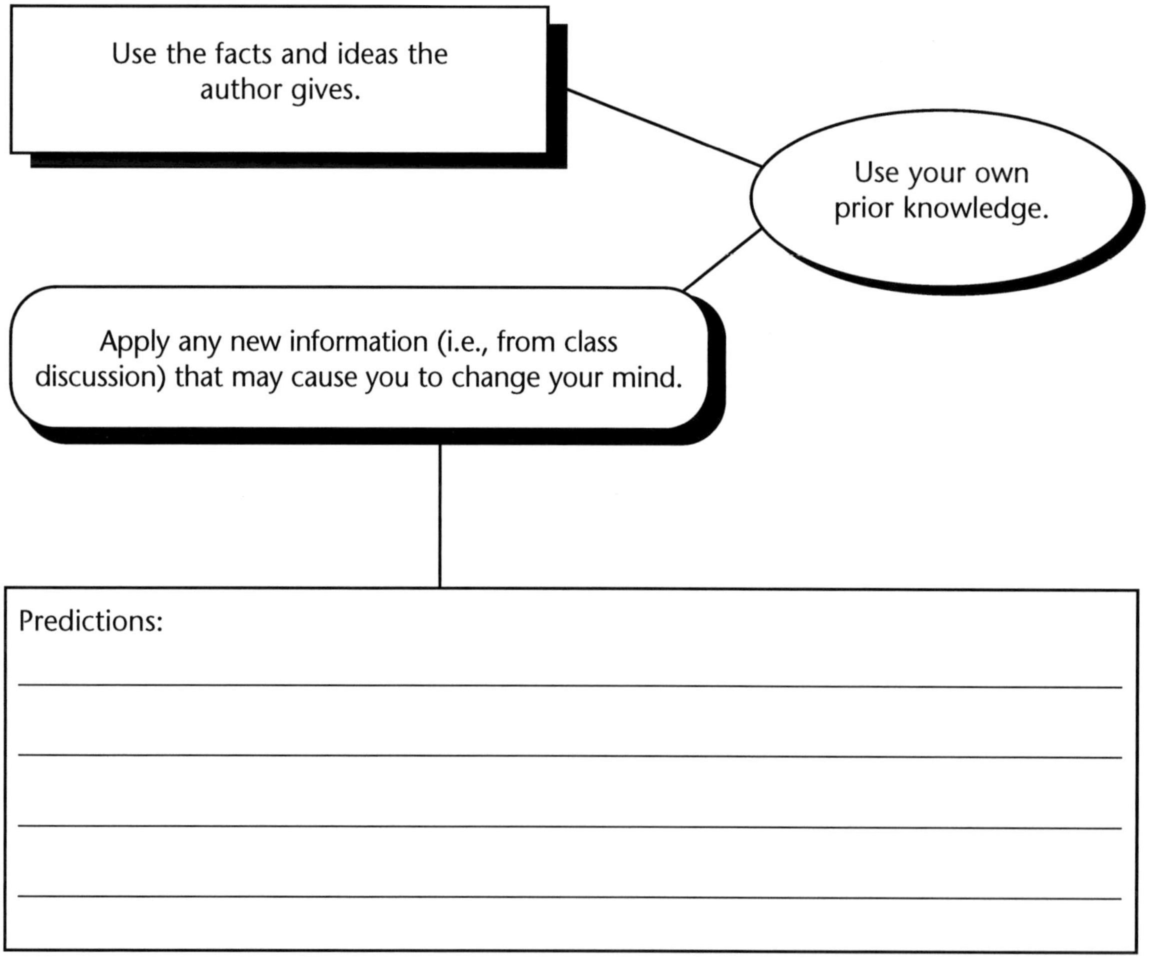

Use the facts and ideas the author gives.

Use your own prior knowledge.

Apply any new information (i.e., from class discussion) that may cause you to change your mind.

Predictions:

Prediction Chart

What characters have we met so far?	What is the conflict in the story?	What are your predictions?	Why did you make those predictions?

Character Chart

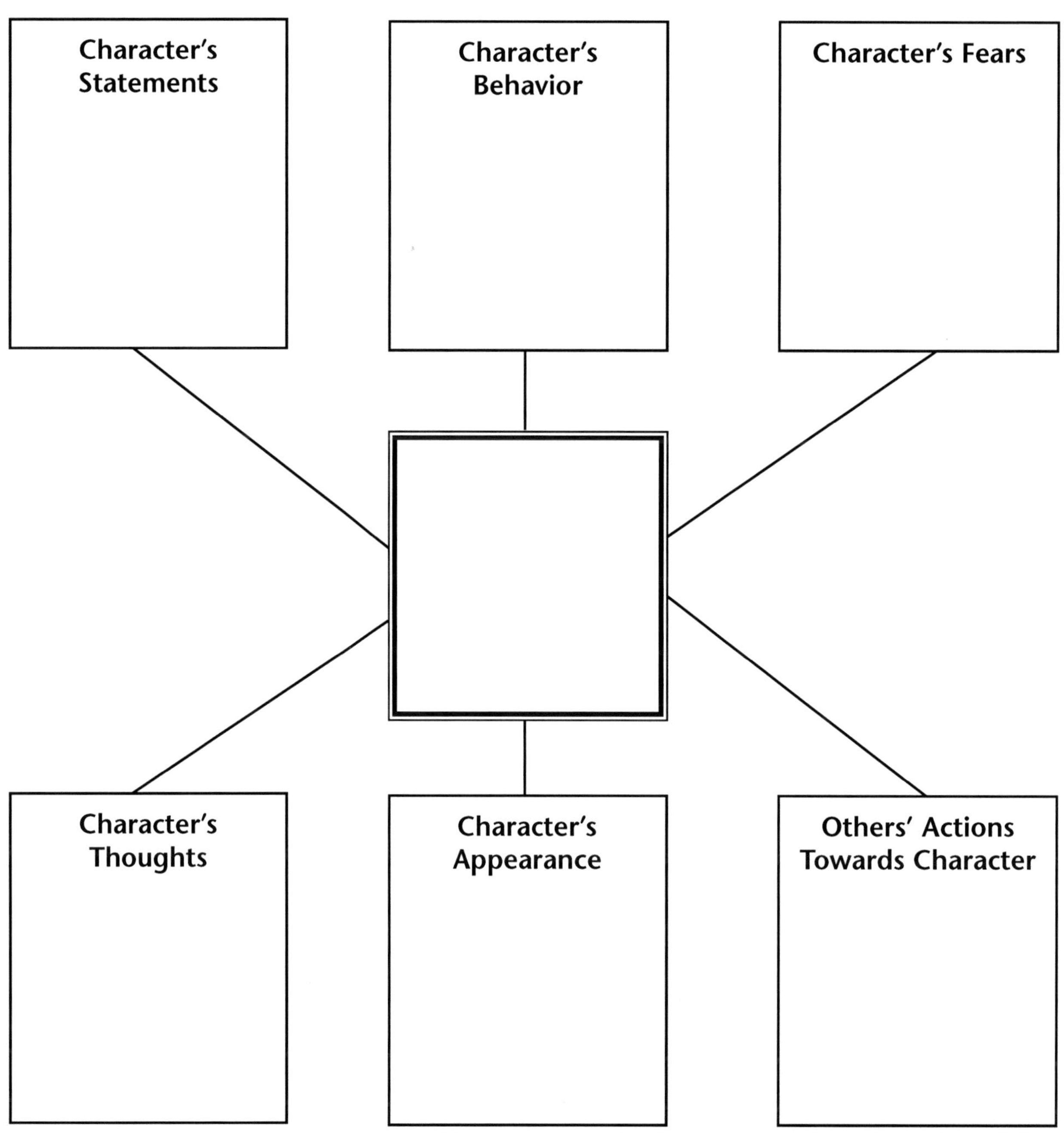

Cause/Effect Chart

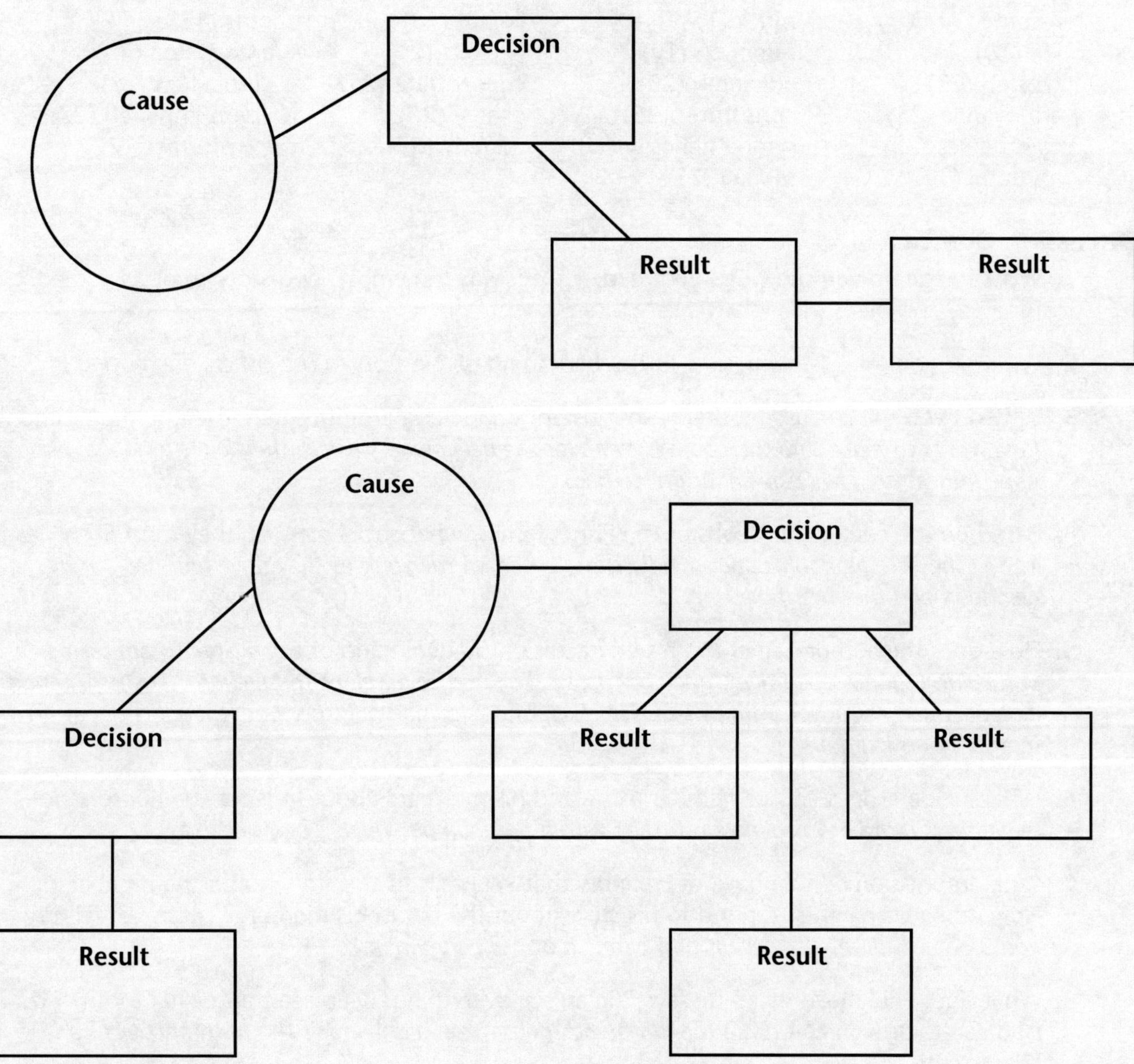

Part 1
August 18-August 23, pp. 1-32

Vocabulary

evidence (1)	receding (2)	predator (2)	prey (3)
hurtling (7)	convoy (7)	citrus (8)	industrial (8)
Coventry (9)	Versailles (9)	wrought-iron (9)	apparently (9)
resumed (14)	muck (15)	lignite (15)	serfs (18)
koi (18)	retention (19)	exploits (21)	anticipated (23)
tension (23)	adjoining (23)	concentrate (25)	curriculum (25)
annoyance (25)	constitutes (25)	osprey (27)	vision-impaired (27)
calisthenics (28)	sympathetically (28)	tragedy (28)	transformed (29)
abruptly (30)	sauna (31)		

Discussion Questions

1. What image do you see when you read, "Like it was the empty, two-story tomb of some runaway zombie"? *(Answers will vary.)*

2. What do you think is happening at the beginning of the story? *(The Fishers are moving.)*

3. Why do you think Paul's mother is so insistent on looking around the house one more time? *(She wants to make sure the house is clean for the new owners before they leave for good. Appearances are obviously important to her.)*

4. Based on the early descriptions of the Fisher family, what social class do they most likely fit into? *(They are probably upper-middle class, based on the vehicles they drive and the neighborhood they live in.)*

5. How does the author depict Mom's character in the beginning of the story? *(Mom seems particular, organized, efficient, and very active. The author develops these characteristics through dialogue, her interaction with other characters, and relaying Paul's personal thoughts about his mother in his journal.)*

6. What incident does Paul remember as he and his mom are about to leave the house? *(He remembers that he was almost attacked with a baseball bat while riding his bike.)*

7. What impression do you have of Erik now that Paul tells us the story about the baseball bat? How do Paul's parents respond to his story about the bat in his memory? *(Answers will vary. Paul's parents dismiss the event and blame it on his poor vision.)*

8. What does Paul mean when he says, "I can see everything. I can see things that Mom and Dad can't. Or won't."? *(Even though he has poor vision, Paul knows the truth about Erik's character.)*

9. How does Paul react when he first sees Florida? *(He has the urge to get out and run through the fields. He thinks it is senseless for people to burn down the trees. Many of his stereotypes about Florida are shattered.)*

10. How does Paul feel about Dad's enthusiasm for Erik's football practices? *(He seems to accept that Dad's major interest in life is Erik's football career.)*

11. What do you think Paul is implying about the "zombie" slowly making its way down Interstate 10? What do you think the zombie symbolizes? *(The problems from their past will soon catch up with them. Answers will vary.)*

12. Why do Paul and his mom think their house is burning? *(Their neighborhood has muck fires every day.)*

13. Why do you think Mom does not tell Mr. Costello what a great football player Erik is? *(She does not want to brag since it is their first meeting.)*

14. Why do you think Erik's football career is so important to Dad? *(Dad regrets never playing football in college and thinks of Erik's success as his own.)*

15. Why does Paul think Mike will change once he gets caught up in the Erik Fisher Football Dream? *(Answers will vary.)*

16. Why do you think Paul is concerned that everyone else is going to make a difference in life? *(The rest of his family are finding their places and Paul isn't sure he knows exactly where he fits in.)*

17. What is the meaning of the following quote? "It's like we are major leaguers who've been sent down to a minor-league city for awhile. We're expected to do great things here and then move back up to the big leagues." *(The neighborhood they live in is small enough that Paul's family, especially his football-playing brother and action-oriented mom, stand out.)*

18. Why do you think Mom doesn't worry or complain about the past? Do you think there are things in Mom's past that she doesn't want to worry about? *(There is no use worrying about a past you cannot change. Answers will vary.)*

19. Why is Paul's mother so concerned about P.E. classes? *(The school doesn't seem to be in good shape nor well-equipped for any sport. Mom knows Paul loves soccer and will want to play on the school's team.)*

20. Why do you think that Paul and his mother keep mentioning the things that Dad overlooked when planning the move to Florida? *(It shows that Dad was mainly concerned with the high school football team's reputation and didn't pay much attention to other important details.)*

21. Paul mentions a huge bird of prey circling overhead. What does this say about Paul's vision literally and symbolically? *(Paul is vision-impaired but can see details other people may miss. Symbolically, he notices a bird of prey, indicating that he can see the difference between that which does and does not prey upon other living things. Answers will vary.)*

22. Do you agree with Paul's idea that, in football, someone comes around in the end and steals all of the glory? *(Answers will vary.)*

23. Why do you think Erik stopped playing soccer? *(He could get more attention playing football.)*

24. What is Paul trying to say when he talks about all the rain and tangerines? *(Answers will vary.)*

25. If Paul is so good at playing soccer, why isn't his father as interested in supporting him as he is Erik? *(He is living vicariously through Erik's football career.)*

Prediction: What will happen to the Fisher family in Tangerine? What problems might the "zombie" Paul talks about symbolize?

Supplementary Activities

1. Writing: The author uses numerous similes and metaphors. Discuss the difference between the two; encourage the students to find at least three of each in the story. Then, ask them to write some of their own based on their own life experiences.

2. Research: The books deals with many different aspects of both soccer and football. Divide the class in half and assign soccer to one group and football to the other. Ask them to research the sport and the positions. Instruct them to come up with a creative way to teach the basics to the class.

3. Discussion: In the novel, Paul and his family have moved numerous times prior to Tangerine County. Ask the students to consider what that might be like. Think about all the different aspects: a new school, new house, new friends, etc. Discuss as a class what Paul and the other members of the family might be feeling. Have students share their own experiences of moving to a new place.

August 28-September 8, pp. 32-64

Vocabulary

torque (33)	identity (34)	incapable (34)	enthusiasm (36)
materializing (38)	ignited (39)	perimeter (40)	benefactor (40)
sergeant (41)	inherited (42)	organizational (42)	irregularities (42)
regulation (42)	shantytown (42)	exaggerating (45)	penalty (46)
samurai (48)	solemnly (49)	singed (49)	comprehend (49)
Mohawked (51)	violent (52)	deliberately (52)	colossal (53)
scrimmage (53)	campaign (54)	destruction (56)	mourn (56)
majority (59)	eligible (61)		

Discussion Questions

1. Why did Erik's friends call Paul "Eclipse Boy"? *(Erik told them that Paul stared into the sun which ruined his eyesight and forced him to wear Coke-bottle glasses.)*

2. What does Paul notice in old family photographs? *(He never wore glasses of any kind before the summer of the eclipse.)*

3. Why does Paul say that teachers and adults value him as an example? *(They use him and his poor eyesight to prove to other children that it is important to do as you are told.)*

4. Why doesn't Paul appreciate the extra help in class due to his vision-impairment? *(Being vision-impaired doesn't make Paul any less of a person.)*
5. Why do you think Paul is so upset about having to follow Kerri around all day long? *(It will make him look and seem helpless to the other students.)*
6. Why are we told that Paul doesn't remember looking at the eclipse? *(It is strange that he doesn't remember. There is probably more to the story.)*
7. How does Paul explain the relationship between the two couples in the backyard? Why are they dating? *(He thinks the boys want to date cheerleaders, and the girls want to date football players. They are more interested in their titles than each other.)*
8. Why do you think that Erik has never expressed an interest in driving? *(Answers will vary.)*
9. Why does Paul think that Arthur will beat out Mike for the job of place-kicker? *(Arthur is becoming Erik's friend and Erik probably has enough influence to choose who will hold the ball for him.)*
10. Why does Paul think Arthur will do anything Erik asks? *(Arthur will want to maintain his chance at fame through Erik, so he will do anything.)*
11. What does Paul realize about Arthur? *(Paul will now be afraid of Arthur as well as Erik.)*
12. Why do you think that Paul has always been afraid of Erik? *(Answers will vary.)*
13. Why do you think that Mom is so obsessed with the regulations in the housing development? *(She likes to be in control, and she wants things to be uniform. She wants the outside of the neighborhood to look good.)*
14. What does the fact that Mom never lived in a nice house have to do with her attitude now? *(She wants to make sure that her children live in a nice house and a nice neighborhood.)*
15. Why do you suppose that Paul has never seen Joey running even though he claims to run every night? *(Joey may not be telling the truth.)*
16. Why does Paul say that the lightning will strike the Donnelly house again? *(He claims that the house is on what used to be the highest spot, and the lightning knows and remembers that.)*
17. What does Paul say will happen one day once all of the houses crumble away and the trees return? *(The storms will make sense again.)*
18. What does Joey tell Paul about lightning? *(He doesn't think it is that complicated, and he doesn't think it knows anything about anything.)*
19. Is Paul good at soccer? What position does he play? *(Yes, he made the team easily; goalie)*
20. What does Erik tell Mom about Mike Costello? *(He died at practice when lightning struck.)*
21. Why does Joey try to take off Mike's shoes? *(Answers will vary.)*

22. Erik and Arthur are laughing about Mike's death. How does this make Paul feel? His mom? What does this say about Erik and Arthur? Discuss. *(Paul is disconcerted; his mom doesn't even notice because she is on the phone with Dad. Erik and Arthur seem cold and heartless. They rejoice about getting a break due to someone's death.)*

23. Paul writes, "Now Mike is dead. But the Dream lives on." What does he mean? *(Even if people die, The Erik Fisher Football Dream will live on in the Fisher house.)*

24. What did the school do in response to Mike's death? *(nothing)*

25. What do you think the school should have done about Mike's death? *(Answers will vary.)*

26. Why does Paul write that if Erik died, he would take his part of the eclipse story with him? *(Paul believes that Erik knows the truth about his eyes. If Erik were to die, Paul would never find out the truth.)*

27. What is the outcome of the meeting? *(They will call all of the parents and move practice to the mornings if that is agreeable.)*

28. What did Coach tell Paul at practice? *(Paul isn't eligible to play, due to his handicap.)*

29. Paul mentions the line of osprey crossing the sky to their nests again. What does Paul think is in the bird's mouth? What might these birds symbolize? *(a koi; answers will vary)*

30. Why does it make Paul feel better to know that his mother is sorry about mentioning his vision? *(He needs to know that she respects how he feels about his eyesight and how it embarrasses him when she makes a big deal out of it, especially when he can see with glasses.)*

Supplementary Activities

1. Science: Have the students do some research on lightning. Have them figure out why Tangerine is struck by lightning so often. Ask them to present their conclusion to the class using visual aids.

2. Debate: Paul mentions a solar eclipse. Have the students research an eclipse. Ask them to decide if they think this could be the cause of Paul's vision problem. Divide the class and have a debate. Instruct the students to have factual information to back up their reasoning.

3. Journals: Have the students respond to the following questions. How do you feel about Erik, knowing that he celebrated Mike's death? How would you feel if Erik were your brother? What would you do about the soccer team if you were in Paul's shoes?

4. Discussion: Ask the students to consider the following questions on their own for ten minutes. How did Dad react to Paul's being kicked off of the team? How would he have responded if Erik had been kicked off the football team? What should Paul do about the situation?

September 8-September 15, pp. 64-92

Vocabulary

Catholic (64)	wake (64)	rosary (66)	migrant workers (71)
magnificent (71)	cathedral (71)	gangstas (72)	pendulum (72)
partitioned (73)	exhibits (73)	Fräulein (73)	affliction (73)
vaulting (79)	chaos (79)	disintegrating (79)	sinkhole (79)
geologist (83)	recapture (83)	agitated (83)	surveys (85)
coincidence (87)	brigade (88)	ominously (89)	conjunction (90)

Discussion Questions

1. Why is it important to Paul to be around Joey? *(Since Joey feels worse than Paul, helping Joey makes Paul's problem seem small in comparison. Paul is being a good friend.)*

2. Why do you think Paul finds it odd that, at the funeral, the conversation with the Costellos is light? *(Answers will vary.)*

3. What does Joey want to ask Paul? *(if he wants to go to the carnival with him)*

4. Why do you think that Paul obsesses about what he could have said to Kerri? *(He likes her and wants her to like him, too.)*

5. Why would it be comforting for Paul to know that something around Tangerine has a history, and that something actually belongs here? *(Answers will vary; Paul wants to know that Tangerine has substance, that everything in it is not fabricated or human-made.)*

6. What does Joey tell Paul about Tangerine Middle? *(The students carry guns and belong to gangs.)*

7. Why do you think that Paul is so fascinated by the people in the freak show? *(He relates to the people in the acts because he thinks that his poor eyesight was caused by some freak accident that he cannot remember.)*

8. Why does Mom get so upset about the kids in the truck? *(None of them are wearing seatbelts.)*

9. Why is Paul called to the office? What does Paul do? *(They are trying to determine who vandalized the "Wonders of the World" show. Paul tells them the culprits were Tangerine Middle soccer players.)*

10. Why do you think Paul is so concerned about ratting on the guys from Tangerine Middle? *(He is used to being around Erik and knows how Erik retaliates when someone rats him out.)*

11. What is happening to all of the portables? *(They are falling into a newly-created sinkhole.)*

12. Discuss the events surrounding the sinkhole. How does the sinkhole affect Paul's life? What might the sinkhole symbolize? *(Paul and Joey help students escape from a sinking portable. Many people are injured. Half of the bleachers at the football stadium sink a little and are condemned, which means the number of fans in the stadium may be smaller at the next football game. The foundation can no longer support all the buildings. CNN covers the story and Paul is disappointed that the sinkhole looks so small. He feels brave for helping students escape. He also will have to go to another school, probably Tangerine Middle. The sinkhole could represent the conflict between humans and nature. Lake Windsor is full of unnatural buildings and lakes. On the surface it looks pleasant, but underneath, it has no depth or support.)*

13. How do you think Paul feels when Gino tells him that the rules about soccer eligibility have been bent for other people in the past? *(He probably feels isolated and irritated by the idea that people think he is too handicapped to play soccer.)*

14. Why does Paul want to go to Tangerine Middle School? *(He wants to play soccer; he won't have an IEP there and will be able to play.)*

15. Do you think Paul means it when he tells his dad that it's okay that he doesn't pay much attention to him? Discuss how much time parents should spend with their children. *(Answers will vary.)*

16. Why does Paul say that the heavens opened up for him? *(He sees the sinkhole as his miracle; because of it he can go to another school and get a chance to play soccer.)*

Supplementary Activities

1. Media: The story told by the media about the sinkhole is different from the actual story. Ask the students to account for these differences. Discuss with them the possibility that the media is monitored and censored. How could this affect the public? What do they think should be done about the possibility?

2. Science: The portables are swallowed up by a sinkhole that is part of a cavern system. Discuss how caverns and sinkholes are created. Use clear pans of dirt, water and straws to show how water can affect the ground. If there is a cavern nearby, this would make a great field trip.

3. Journals: When disaster strikes, Paul jumps in to help. Ask the students to consider what they would do in an emergency situation.

Part 2
September 18-September 22, pp. 95-123

Vocabulary

menacing (95)	impression (95)	disinfectant (99)	inconsistent (103)
integer (104)	offense (106)	defense (106)	combatants (108)
jeering (115)	frenzy (115)	intimidation (115)	mercifully (117)
upended (117)	unobstructed (118)	berserk (119)	momentum (120)

Discussion Questions

1. Why do none of the buildings in Tangerine have three floors other than the school? *(Answers will vary.)*

2. What does Paul mean when he says that Tangerine Middle is like a mirror universe to Lake Windsor? Discuss the differences and whether or not Paul feels comfortable at Tangerine Middle. *(Everything is the same concerning the course of the school day. However, the people are very different; the minorities are the majority; Paul feels like he fits in because he always saw himself as a minority. He is a little nervous in the halls sometimes but excited about playing for the champion soccer team.)*

3. What do you think will happen when the suspended guys from the soccer team meet Paul? Will they recognize him? *(Answers will vary.)*

4. Why is Paul is willing to play second string? *(He is happy to be playing soccer at all.)*

5. What happened to Paul's IEP? *(Mom got rid of the IEP before she delivered his file to Tangerine Middle.)*

6. Why do you think Paul decides to try to make a joke with Victor? *(to break the ice; he decides to mock Lake Windsor so they recognize that he is glad to be at Tangerine Middle)*

7. Why is Paul so interested in the story of how the boys got in trouble at the carnival? *(He wants to see if they know that he ratted on them and finally realizes they don't know who it was.)*

8. What do you think about the Tangerine Middle team after hearing how Victor scored the goal on Paul? *(They are tough and do not readily welcome outsiders.)*

9. What do Arthur and Erik do while Joey is at the Fisher's house? *(They make fun of Joey and his deceased brother, Mike.)*

10. Why was Joey trying to get Mike's shoes off? Does he care that no one else understood? *(It was the only thing Joey could think to do; Mike always felt better when he took his shoes off at home. Joey cared more about his brother than anyone else at the time. Answers will vary.)*

11. What does Paul try to get Joey to do? *(go to school at Tangerine Middle)*

12. What does the coach mean when she says, "There's no way this team can beat you. You can only beat yourselves."? *(They are a good team and will win if they play well.)*

13. What happens to Paul's eyes while he is playing? How does his team respond? *(One of the other players smears mud in them. Later, Victor tells him that if he is a War Eagle, no one will ever mess with him.)*

14. Why does Paul want Theresa to show Joey around on Monday? *(She has connections because she is Tino's sister. In order to be protected and make friends at Tangerine, you have to have tough friends. They will only befriend you if they do not consider you to be an outsider.)*

15. What are the differences between the students who attend Lake Windsor and the students who attend Tangerine Middle? *(Answers will vary. Lake Windsor students are more independent than Tangerine students seem to be. At Tangerine, groups stick together tighter than in Lake Windsor.)*

Prediction: How will Joey handle going to school at Tangerine Middle? Will he fit in?

Supplementary Activities

1. Journals: Paul talks about the first impression he gets when he walks into Tangerine Middle. Ask the students to recall the first time they walked into their school, the first time they met their teachers for the year, and a few other first impressions. Ask them whether these first impressions proved to be true. Ask them to think about what kind of first impression they make on people. Are first impressions important?
2. Physical Education: Study the rules of soccer. Assign each student a position to reasearch. Begin playing soccer as a team. Discuss some of the things that were done incorrectly in the game against Palmetto.
3. History: Have the students research the origin and development of soccer, noting any changes as the sport evolved. Have the students think about what attending a soccer game might be like in other countries, for example: the fans' enthusiasm, the attitude of the players, the playing conditions, etc.

September 23-October 4, pp. 123-155

Vocabulary

hyper (123)	milling (123)	pantomiming (124)	squadron (124)
surrendered (124)	two-point conversion (127)	decoy (128)	condemned (128)
humiliation (129)	opponents (129)	lobbed (133)	recovered (133)
assault (133)	eager (134)	scarce (134)	stunned (135)
scamming (136)	extension (136)	inescapable (137)	maniacs (138)
initiation (139)	circumstances (140)	disruptive (143)	cross-curricular (144)
agriculture (144)	doubtfully (146)	laden (148)	resistant (148)
prominence (148)	registered (148)	variety (148)	industry (149)
sarcastically (150)	lunged (150)	alcove (151)	fax modem (151)
navigator (151)	gourmet (153)	saturating (153)	encephalitis (153)
insecticide (154)	pesticide (154)	delicate (154)	exterminator (154)
liable (154)	dilapidated (155)	glumly (155)	adjourn (155)

Discussion Questions

1. How do you think Mom feels about Erik having to play in the afternoon rainstorm? *(She is unhappy. That is exactly what she was trying to stop by moving practice to another time.)*
2. Do you think Erik is as excited about the way the game turned out as Dad is? *(No, Erik ends up looking like a fool. He isn't a team player. He wants all of the credit and doesn't get any.)*

3. Why doesn't Arthur congratulate Antoine for his two-point conversion? *(Arthur knows that Erik is not happy about it, and he wouldn't do anything to upset Erik.)*

4. Why does Paul think that someone is going to pay for Erik's humiliation? *(Erik is not used to being made fun of, and he will probably blame and punish Antoine for his embarrassment.)*

5. Why does Paul think that his parents would watch him play if he played football instead of soccer? *(His parents care about Erik's football. His dad used to play football; he would like to think that thier fascination is with the game rather than with Erik.)*

6. How do you think Paul feels when he realizes that he scored a goal? (*proud and happy)*

7. Why is Paul surprised when Cara calls him? *(Girls in the past probably didn't pay much attention to him.)*

8. Why do you think Paul is shocked when he realizes that Kerri likes him? *(It is unusual; Erik is usually the one who gets attention in his family. He finds it hard to believe that anyone could possibly be interested in him.)*

9. How do you think Joey should have handled Victor when he was giving him a hard time? How should Paul have acted? *(Answers will vary.)*

10. Can you think of a reason why Shandra runs away when Dolly tells her that the reporters want to talk to her? *(Answers will vary.)*

11. Why does Joey think that Tino is bad news? *(Answers will vary; Tino likes picking on Joey.)*

12. Why doesn't Paul feel the same way about Tino? *(Tino already picked on him, but he has learned how to get along with Tino and his group. He knows they are not always mean and that when you are their friend, they will protect you and take care of you. Paul doesn't think less of Tino because he goes to Tangerine or doesn't have as much money as his family does.)*

13. Compare and contrast Tino and Joey. *(Answers will vary; Joey is used to Lake Windsor where people have more money and he is part of the majority. At Tangerine, Joey is a minority. He isn't used to the tough nature of Tangerine and doesn't think highly of the people who go there. Tino is extremely loyal to his group of friends and family. He is a minority, but has made a name for himself at Tangerine and will protect it. He doesn't think highly of people who come from the richer school, Lake Windsor. They both have prejudices against one another, are both Paul's friends, and like soccer.)*

14. What is happening at Paul's house while he is trying to work at the computer? What is everyone talking about? *(a homeowner's association meeting; termite and mosquito problems and robberies)*

15. What could all of the neighborhood's problems symbolize? *(Everyone lives in nice homes, but everything under the surface is rotten; an example of humans vs. nature; cannot put out muck fires, only create more problems; problems come from things the people themselves do)*

16. What does Paul contribute to the meeting? How does this contribute to the theme concerning sight in the story? *(Paul has observed ospreys taking the koi out of the lake. He knows a person isn't responsible for it. None of the adults ever noticed. It is ironic that Paul notices this because he has vision problems.)*

17. What did Paul find on his father's computer? *(a file containing information on Erik's scholarship offers)*

Prediction: What will happen as a result of all of the robberies in the neighborhood?

Supplementary Activities

1. Problem Solving: Have the students develop actual solutions to the various problems the homeowners of Lake Windsor are facing. Encourage them to write their plans down and to carefully think of how they would carry out each solution. Have them present their ideas to the class and discuss which ideas would work the best.

2. Personal Narrative: Paul is extremely proud of scoring in the soccer game. Have the students think of a proud moment in their life. Ask them to write a personal narrative recreating the event.

3. Classroom Building: Write a list of the names of each student in the class on the board. Ask each student to copy the list on their own paper and to omit their own name from the list. Encourage each student to write at least three positive things to say about each student. Only one comment can be based on physical appearances. Take up these papers and create a list of "positives" for each student.

October 5-November 10, pp. 156-194

Vocabulary

re-enrolling (156), Quonset hut (158), nursery (159), rootstock (160), grafted (160), scion (160), generator (161), avalanche (164), collided (165), statistics (165), rampage (165), whooping (165), bandolera (166), intensely (168), reverence (168), critical (168), aerosol (168), horticulture (170), conscience (170), frantically (173), capsizing (173), composed (173), genuinely (173), interjected (175), boycott (175), amateur (176), resumed (177), congregated (178), forfeit (179), destiny (180), archenemy (182), hostile (183), sincerely (183), granted (183), veered (184), intent (186), retaliate (186), catapulted (192), vehemently (192), spectators (192), commotion (194)

Discussion Questions

1. Why does Paul think that Joey isn't at school? *(He thinks Joey is re-enrolling at Lake Windsor Middle.)*

2. Do you think that Joey belongs at Lake Windsor like Paul said? Why? *(Joey is more judgmental than Paul about people who are different from him. He prefers being around people who do not look down on him because he is from Lake Windsor and who are from a higher social class.)*

3. Why do you think Tino ignores Paul? Will he treat him as a friend again? *(Answers will vary.)*
4. Do you think Paul is truly interested in the tangerine business? *(Answers will vary.)*
5. Why do you think that Paul's parents did not notice that he was crying while they were checking his peripheral vision? *(Answers will vary.)*
6. What kinds of things does Paul say he can see with his new glasses that his parents can't see? What does Paul mean? *(Paul sees Erik posing in front of his parents, the star of the Football Dream. He can also see Erik lurking behind him. Somehow, Paul sees the cruelty in Erik that his parents try to deny.)*
7. Why doesn't Paul write in his journal for four weeks? *(The Fisher family is more involved in the community, including Paul with his soccer and school. They are not around each other a lot.)*
8. What does Paul mean and what is he referring to when he says that they are all becoming big fish in a little pond? *(They are all becoming significant people in their small community.)*
9. How is soccer affecting Paul's life right now? *(His team is winning. Other teams fear the War Eagles and Paul is excited to be intimidating rather than intimidated.)*
10. Why does Paul go back to the tangerine orchard? What significant events happen there? Discuss Tino's behavior. *(Paul wants to go and knows Luis really meant he could come back. He becomes friends with Tino, who treats Paul as a friend because Paul shows an interest in him and his family.)*
11. Why did Paul want to clear his conscience about ratting on the boys? *(He feels guilty since they are now his friends.)*
12. Why is Paul's family shocked when they hear Mr. Donnelly say that he is pleased to meet Paul? *(No one ever seems to care if they meet Paul, only Erik.)*
13. Discuss Paul's flashback to his old garage. Why is this significant? *(We learn how badly Paul's eyes were hurt. It seems odd that his mom doesn't want him to tell his grandparents anything.)*
14. How do you think Paul will feel when he plays against his old friends at Lake Windsor Middle? *(Answers will vary.)*
15. What does Paul mean when he says he was now looking at his surroundings through the hostile eyes of a War Eagle? *(Answers will vary.)*
16. What does Paul mean when he says that the homes in Lake Windsor are as phony as the Erik Fisher Football Hero Smile? *(It is all superficial—pretty only on the surface.)*
17. What does the coach mean when she says, "If you retaliate, you're playing their game. If you get focused on soccer, you're playing our game"? *(They need to play the game the way they were taught and not get hung up in all the foolishness of fighting.)*
18. What does Coach Walski try to do to Paul? *(He wants Paul taken out of the game because he lives in a different school district.)*

19. What does Coach Bright inform him about Shandra? *(Her brother is Antoine Thomas who goes to Lake Windsor even though he should go to Tangerine.)*
20. How do you think Paul feels when Gino says that Paul is the reason he missed the shot? *(Paul should feel like he is a powerful player.)*
21. Why do you think Paul tells his mother that she will have to follow the bus back to Tangerine? *(He wants to be with his team after the last game; they are his friends. It doesn't seem like an unreasonable request.)*
22. Why is Paul crying when he gets off of the bus? *(It is his last game at Tangerine Middle.)*
23. What do you think he is talking about when he tells Mom that it was "quite a ride"? *(everything that had happened to him recently)*

Supplementary Activities

1. Science: Luis teaches the boys about how to create new trees by grafting them onto rough lemon trees. Encourage the students to do some research about how this works. Then, ask them to create some sort of plant that they think would be useful in their society. Make sure they explain how and why they would create the plant. They should illustrate what the product and the tree would look like.
2. Debate: Paul wonders if Coach Bright minds the publicity that is created by reopening the issue regarding her and the Olympics. Some people believe that the public has the right to know all sorts of things about anyone who is captured on film. Other people think that it is rude and inappropriate to publish information about someone without his or her consent. Split the class in half. Ask them to research the idea, and then have a classroom debate over the issue.
3. History: Henry D. tells Paul about the Quonset huts that some of the tangerine farmers bought from the government after the war. Ask the students to do some research to discover if this is true. Ask them to turn their findings into some sort of product. For example: a poster with illustrations and captions, a story explaining the history of the huts, or a commercial advertising one to a person interested in buying one from the government.

Part 3
November 20-November 24, pp. 197-230

Vocabulary

neglected (197)	mesmerized (198)	insolently (199)	contort (199)
sorrow (199)	agonizing (201)	accompanying (201)	hoist (202)
guidance (203)	incident (203)	cautiously (204)	unflinching (208)
potential (212)	withering (215)	scorched (216)	revolting (216)
emphasis (216)	corrugated (216)	amputated (218)	obediently (219)
deliberately (225)			

Discussion Questions

1. How does Erik treat Paul's group when they visit the house? Why does Erik insult them? *(Erik taunts them and insults them. When they talk back to him, he hits Tino hard enough to draw blood. Answers will vary.)*

2. How does Paul describe Erik's hand? *(a slow, casual snake)*

3. What impression do you get of Erik when he tells Arthur that they won't be needing whatever it is that Arthur pulled out of his gym bag? *(Arthur pulls out a weapon of some sort that will seriously injure someone. The way they talk about using a weapon is scary and intimidating.)*

4. What does Paul see in Erik's eyes after Erik hits Tino? Why does Erik look at him that way? *(sorrow or fear; answers will vary)*

5. Do you think Dad watched the whole episode? How should Paul and his parents have reacted? *(Answers will vary.)*

6. What do you think will happen to Paul's friendships now that Erik hit Tino? *(Answers will vary.)*

7. What does Paul mean when he says that he is "sick to his soul"? *(He is so disturbed by Erik's behavior emotionally and mentally that it makes him physically nauseous.)*

8. Why is Paul not able to rat on Erik? *(His parents never punish Erik. They deny he is the "psycho" Paul believes he is.)*

9. Why do you think that Erik asks for a key to the storage shed? *(Answers will vary.)*

10. Why does Paul worry about whether Mom and Dad will like what he has to say? *(He knows they live in denial about Erik and doesn't want to worry them if they won't punish Erik anyway.)*

11. Why does Paul decide that Erik's hitting Tino is not something that Mom needs to know about? *(He figures she won't do anything about it anyway.)*

12. Why do you think that Erik told Mom that he would have to bring the key home from school? *(He is stalling. It is suspicious that he even needs a key at all.)*

13. What does Paul decide to do to help Luis and his family? *(He wants to help them fight the freeze.)*

14. Why do you think that everyone is so surprised and concerned about Paul? *(Paul is Erik's brother. After Erik hits Tino, it is bold of Paul to come help the Cruz family. They are concerned because he is not used to the cold weather, and they know they will have to watch him closely.)*

15. Mom is silent on the phone. Why might she be acting weird? Why does she talk to Paul about trust? *(Someone may have violated her trust. Answers will vary.)*

16. Do you think something happened at the storage shed? If so, what? Why do you think so? *(Mom acts strange on the phone and mentions she got into the building without Erik's key; therefore, she went in before Erik.)*

17. What do Paul and Luis talk about? *(Erik; Paul tells Luis what he saw Arthur do to him; Luis warns Paul that something will happen to change Erik's attitude on Monday.)*

18. Why is Paul humiliated when he wakes up in the hut? *(All the others worked through the night, but he had to sleep inside where it was warm.)*

19. Describe the difference between how Erik and Paul treat people. *(Erik–destructive, cruel, secretive, selfish, bully; Paul–helpful, kind, accepting; Erik hurts others while Paul helps others.)*

20. Why do you think that Brian Baylor was unable to snap the ball during the big game? *(He didn't want Erik to be able to kick the field goals.)*

21. Why isn't Shandra's picture in the paper? *(They do not want any connections made to her and Antoine since he goes to the wrong school.)*

22. What do you think happened to Paul while he was outside? *(Answers will vary.)*

23. What does Paul mean when he says that he cannot remember why he feels so weird, at least "not yet"? *(Perhaps he is beginning to remember something that happened to him in the past.)*

Prediction: Will Paul remember something strange that happened to him in the past? What will it be?

Prediction: How will Erik and Arthur get a "new attitude" on Monday?

Supplementary Activities

1. Journals: Ask the students to imagine that they are in Paul's shoes. What should he have done when Erik began to approach Tino? What about when Luis approached Erik? Is there anything he should have done differently? Should Paul have told his parents? Why or why not?

2. Science: Paul goes to help Luis fight the freeze. Ask the students to research the many different ways that farmers have to deal with the weather. Separate the students into groups. Assign each group a location and a product to study, for example: Central Texas and hay. Ask them to determine what farmers must do in the climate specific to their location and with their product. Ask them to turn their projects into presentations for the class.

3. Art: Paul gives a detailed description of what the tangerine groves look like while they are trying to fight the freeze. Ask the students to create an illustration based on the information given in the story.

November 27-December 2, pp. 230-262

Vocabulary

mutual (230)	despised (230)	gestured (236)	frazzled (236)
aneurysm (237)	sterile (238)	persistent (238)	electrocuted (242)
murky (243)	wail (248)	descending (248)	mirage (249)
pummeling (250)	bellowed (250)	prostrate (251)	recede (254)
apparition (254)			

Discussion Questions

1. How does Paul know something goes wrong on Monday? What do you think Paul hoped would happen? *(Erik is acting normally and doesn't look beat up; answers will vary.)*
2. Why do you think that Paul accepts Kerri's offer to go to Joey's? *(Perhaps Paul wants to see Joey again. He is excited about going as Kerri's date.)*
3. Who figures out what is happening to the fish? Why is this significant? *(Paul has seen the osprey flying away with the fish. Again, this shows how Paul sees things adults do not see.)*
4. What goes through Paul's head when he hears that Luis' aneurysm was caused by a blow to the head? *(He thinks that Arthur and Erik are responsible for killing Luis.)*
5. Why didn't anything happen to Erik and Arthur on Monday? *(Luis was already dead.)*
6. Why does Paul think he is just as guilty as Erik? *(He chose not to tell anyone about what he saw.)*
7. What does Paul mean when he says that Luis' family knows the truth; their lives are not built around bits and pieces of the truth? *(Paul's life is built on only pieces of truth where people see and believe only what they want. His parents only half-believe and half-listen to the truth all the time. The Luis family isn't afraid of facing reality, even if it doesn't portray the best image.)*
8. Why do you think Paul starts to yell at the little boy? *(Paul is frustrated with the lies his parents have told him about Erik. He is beginning to realize that all his life, his parents made excuses for Erik and people suffered, even died, because of it.)*
9. Do you think Luis' family grew up hearing the same stories? Why or why not? *(Probably not; they were told the truth about why you should avoid certain things. That is why their lives are so different from Paul's.)*
10. Why do you think that Paul's ritual in the backyard made him feel closer to Luis? *(Answers will vary. The recognition of the earth and the truth it produces may make him feel like he can better understand and appreciate Luis, even in his death.)*
11. Who does Paul see when he looks toward the entrance during the ceremony? *(Tino and Victor)*
12. What do you think Tino and Victor are planning to do? *(Answers will vary.)*
13. What does Paul mean when he says that Tino and Victor are staring with the "wrath of God"? *(They want justice for Luis' death and are willing to do what it takes to humiliate and injure Erik and Arthur.)*
14. Why do you think that Tino and Victor chose to attack Erik and Arthur in such a public place? *(They want everyone to see them avenge Luis' death; they want to humiliate them.)*

15. Why, for the first time, is Paul no longer afraid of Erik? *(Answers will vary.)*

16. Discuss what really happened to Paul's eyes. Is it surprising that Erik is responsible? How does the author prepare the readers for this revelation? *(Paul's eyes were injured when Erik's friend sprayed Paul's eyes with paint with Erik there. That Erik is responsible is not a surprise because we have seen the way he treats other people, his cold-heartedness, and his hatred for Paul. We are also prepared because of Paul's other flashbacks and innate fear of his brother.)*

17. Do you think Mom was aware of what happened to Paul's eyes? If so, why hasn't she told him? Why did they treat Erik so wonderfully if he is responsible for Paul's blindness? *(Answers will vary.)*

18. How did Mom and Dad handle the spray paint situation? Is there a better way? *(They never tell Paul what really happened and do not punish Erik. They don't want Paul to hate Erik. They should have told Paul, or at least punished Erik in some way. Answers will vary.)*

19. Is it good that Paul remembers what really happened to him? Why or why not? *(The truth frees Paul, like Antoine said. He wishes his parents would have told him. Answers will vary.)*

20. Why do you think that Antoine is at Mr. Donnelly's house with Coach Bright? *(Answers will vary.)*

Prediction: What is the important meeting going to be about tomorrow? Why is Erik "hiding his face"?

Supplementary Activities

1. Peresusasive Writing: Ask the students to consider if it is better to know the truth even if it is painful. Ask them if they would rather live with a lie if it seemed to make life easier. Ask the students to consider the options and take a side. Have them write a paper defending their position.

2. Research: At one point Paul is afraid he is just as guilty as Erik for Luis' death since he didn't tell anyone. Ask the students to research the laws and determine if Paul has done wrong by keeping the truth a secret. What do they think he should have done? What types of punishment do Erik and Arthur face?

3. Journals: Shandra talks about how hard it is for Antoine to play against some of his old friends. Students should write a journal entry explaining why they think Antoine misses the awards ceremony. Would it truly be worth the fame to play against their friends? What would they do in the situation?

4. Science: Luis died of an aneurysm. Explain to the students exactly what an aneurysm is, and explain what sort of things might cause one to become fatal. Ask them how they feel about Erik and Arthur, knowing that their actions helped to kill Luis.

December 3-December 6, pp. 262-294

Vocabulary

territorial (263) boundaries (263) nullify (263) drastic (263)
notarized (263) immortality (265) miraculously (266) dominant (267)
shards (267) strategy (268) complied (269) ogre (270)
restitution (272) unanimous (272) disclosure (273) mannequins (273)
reluctantly (274) medicated (278) weary (280) acreage (281)
violation (285) realization (286) notorious (289) unprecedented (289)
severed (290)

Discussion Questions

1. What was in the paper? *(The story of how Antoine had been attending the wrong school.)*

2. What spurs Antoine to action and what does he do? *(Luis dies and Antoine realizes that things have gone too far. He comes clean about playing football in the wrong district and tells the truth. He also tells what he witnessed when Arthur hit Luis on the football field.)*

3. Now that the Sports Commission has nullified all games that Antoine was involved in, what will happen to the Erik Fisher Football Dream? *(It disappears; Erik's chances of getting a football scholarship are destroyed.)*

4. What is Mr. Donnelly trying to say in his own article? *(Antoine Thomas is the greatest player ever to come out of Tangerine County, and no matter what the Sports Commission does, nothing will change that fact.)*

5. What does Paul tell his father about eyesight (p. 268)? *(He makes Dad admit the truth about his life. Dad has been living a lie becuse he has ignored Erik's true character. Dad also knows the truth about Antoine.)*

6. Discuss how Mom, Dad, and Mr. and Mrs. Bauer handle the meeting about the stolen items. Do you agree or disagree with the way they handle the situation? *(They are returning all the stolen items and pleading for the victims to not press charges and to give their sons a second chance. Answers will vary.)*

7. Do you think that the boys should be punished? *(Answers will vary.)*

8. Why are the cops are looking for Arthur? *(They suspect he is involved in Luis' death.)*

9. Why do you think Paul chooses to tell the police all the information? How do truth and lies function in the story? *(He is tired of all the lying. Truth reflects the realities the people must face while lies reflect the façades people put on to hide what is real.)*

10. Why do you think Grandpop tells Mom that the house is beautiful and not anything like any of the houses he made her live in? *(He is letting her know that no matter what kind of home she lives in, she cannot mask what lives on the inside.)*

11. Why does Theresa think that Paul has messed up his whole life by coming to her school? *(He could have gone to the rich school but instead he went to a school where she thinks he doesn't belong. She probably doesn't think that he will ever be able to go back to his old life.)*

12. What happens to Paul, Tino, and Victor? Are they given fair punishment? *(Tino and Victor get suspended for three days because they hit a student. Because Paul jumped on an employee, he is expelled. Answers will vary. Point out that the rules were not bent for Paul like they always were for Erik.)*

13. Why is it so important to Paul that he is going to be feared? *(He has feared Erik his whole life; he doesn't know what it is like to have someone fear him.)*

14. How does Mom and Dad's behavior toward Paul change? How is this significant? *(Mom and Dad begin treating Paul better, as evidenced by his mom buying him all new clothes. His dad begins taking him to school and developing a relationship with his younger son—and it isn't even based on football.)*

15. Why is it important that Tino calls Paul? *(It shows that Paul has finally been accepted by a group, regardless of where and how they live. Paul has true friends.)*

16. What does Paul mean about the cage that Erik created for himself? *(Everything that has gone wrong in Erik's life is his own fault.)*

17. What does Paul think about Mike's tree? (*He thinks it is nice that Mike has one tree, but Luis has many trees that will live on and on.)*

18. What scent does Paul smell as he is going to school? *(a golden dawn)*

19. What is he referring to? *(Luis' tangerines)*

Supplementary Activities

1. Reflection: Arthur's parents and Erik's parents both try to get the boys out of trouble for stealing in the neighborhood. Ask the students to consider if the parents are helping or hurting the boys. What lesson are they teaching them by helping them out of the situation? What do the students think their parents would do if faced with the same problem? What would the students do if they had children?

2. Literary Analysis: Much of this story has to do with people's attitudes. Ask the students to consider how Paul's attitude changes throughout the story. What about Mom's, Dad's, and Erik's attitudes?

3. Metaphor: Mr. Donnelly refers to his record as a porcelain plate. Once the record is broken it becomes a broken plate that no amount of glue can fix. Ask the students to come up with a metaphor describing something in their life. Encourage them to come up with an illustration to help explain their metaphor. Ask them to share the finished product with the class.

4. Class Discussion: Encourage the students to pretend that they are on the Sports Commission. Ask them to come up with reasons to support nullifying all of the games in which Antoine was involved. Ask them to come up with other solutions. As a class, discuss the best option. Discuss whether their outcome is the same as the story's.

Post-reading Discussion Questions

1. How do each of the characters change as the story progresses?
2. What do you imagine Paul's life will be like now?
3. How do you think the family is going to deal with Erik's crimes?
4. How do you feel about the ruling made by the Sports Commission to nullify all games involving Antoine Thomas?
5. Why do you think Paul is always surprised to know that other people like him?
6. Discuss the difference between being famous and being a good person.
7. Who is more successful, Erik or Paul? Why?
8. Is Erik ever a true friend to anyone? Is Paul? Why or why not?
9. What do you think will happen to The Erik Fisher Football Dream?
10. Is Paul a nerd, as he claims? Why or why not?
11. What lessons do you think Paul's parents have learned?
12. Evaluate who is truly blind and truly able to see throughout the book. Who is most able to see the truth? Why?

Post-reading Extension Activities

1. There are many ways to describe characters in a story. A *round character* is a character that we know many things about. Think of the term well-rounded. A *flat character* is one that we only know one or two things about. We do not get to know a flat character very well. A *dynamic character* is a character that changes throughout the course of the book. A *static character* stays the same throughout the entire novel. Use these four terms to describe the following characters: Paul, Erik, Mom, Dad, Joey, Victor, Tino, Luis, Arthur, Antoine and any other characters in which you are particularly interested. Be sure to explain your answers fully, and use examples from the story to support your ideas.

2. Create small discussion groups. Direct one person to be the leader and encourage him/her to keep the group on task and come up with discussion questions for the group. Direct another person to illustrate what s/he believes to be one of the most important events in the story. Another group member should find a section of the novel that s/he feels needs to be re-discussed. Assign another person the job of pointing out how the lessons of the story can be applied to daily life. Once everyone has completed their assigned job, begin the discussion. Each person should have something to share and discuss with the group.

3. Pick the character in which you are most interested. Create a collage that expresses that character. Try to be as creative as possible. The idea behind the collage is that you have created a summary of the novel and the character just by using pictures and images. Share your collage with the class.

4. As a class, hold a mock trial for Erik. Be sure to include all necessary people, lawyers, judge, jury, defendants, family members, witnesses, etc. Try to make this as real as possible. Encourage the jury to do some legal research in order to make a decision about punishment.

5. Pick a character from the story. Map the main events the character is involved in. It might be helpful to begin with a character chart. What causes different things to happen to the character? What do these cause/effect relationships reveal about the character? (See pp. 8-9 of this guide.)

6. Mr. Donnelly writes about an imaginary porcelain plate that has his football record inscribed on it. What have you done that you are extremely proud of? In what way would you display that information?

7. We are told over and over that Luis and his family have a tangerine farm, and their lives are very different from Paul's. Exactly how are they different? Create a Venn diagram expressing the similarities and differences.

8. When Paul arrives in Florida he expects to see beaches and condos. This is a stereotype that he has learned. Think about other stereotypes you are aware of. Are there any in the book? List stereotypes on a posterboard and decide if they are accurate.

9. There are many things that Paul wants to say to his parents but never has the courage to. Pretend that you are Paul and write a letter expressing all the things you want your parents to know. Include an explanation for why you have never told them these things before.

10. Create a list of the ten questions that you think are most important in understanding the story's message. Share these questions with the class.

11. Look back through the story and map out the weather. Can you find any foreshadowing or symbolism? What part does the weather play in the story?

12. Have a class discussion about the importance and irony of Paul's vision impairment. Why is it such a large part of the story? Why do different characters assign different levels of severity to the problem? How would the story be different if Paul had perfect vision?

Assessment for *Tangerine*

Assessment is an ongoing process. The following 15 items can be completed during the novel study. Once finished, the student and teacher will check the work. Points may be added to indicate the level of understanding.

Name ______________________________ Date ______________

Student	Teacher	
______	______	1. Write a conversation that Paul might have with Erik now that he is no longer afraid of him.
______	______	2. Create a board game that expresses the main events of the story.
______	______	3. Pick a character (other than Paul) and create diary entries from that character's perspective concerning at least three events.
______	______	4. Create a scrapbook of items that Paul might have created in order to remember his seventh grade year.
______	______	5. Write a letter to the author expressing your views on the story.
______	______	6. Create a test that will appropriately check for understanding of the story. Include the answers as well.
______	______	7. Pretend you are the author and continue the story. What will happen to Paul, Erik, Mom, Dad, etc. next year?
______	______	8. Create an advertisement for the book.
______	______	9. If you were to turn the book into a movie, who would you choose to play each character? Why?
______	______	10. Create a musical collage expressing the main emotions and ideas in the story.
______	______	11. With a partner, act out a scene from the novel.
______	______	12. Compare/contrast Paul's personality to your own.
______	______	13. Choose an event in the novel and explain how each of the characters reacted.
______	______	14. Write a poem about the book.
______	______	15. Research and create a poster explaining how to graft a tree.

Notes